I0212712

When The Mouth Can't Speak
The Body Will

poems and pictures

Jane Herschlag

Finishing Line Press
Georgetown, Kentucky

When The Mouth Can't Speak The Body Will

ACKNOWLEDGMENTS

I would like to thank the publishers of the following poems: Doctor When
You Speak/*Metaphors*; Father Slavering/*Bully in the Spotlight*; Fish and
Tackle/*The Returning Woman*; I Dream of Irises/*Muse Press*; It's Taken Five
Decades/*Graffiti Rag*; Trapped/*Moon Journal*; Why Don't Doctors Know?/
Bully in the Spotlight

I also want to thank my husband for encouraging my writing and editing,
my twin for paying for my first writing class and loving my poems, my
wonderful professors, mentors, and writing retreat hosts who gave me
scholarships at: Skidmore College; Wesleyan University; Juniper Summer
Writing Institute, and Fine Arts Writing Center.

Publisher: Leah Maines
Editor: Christen Kincaid
Cover Art and Design: Herbert Herschlag
Author Photo: Herbert Herschlag

Printed in the USA on acid-free paper.
Order online: www.finishinglinepress.com
also available on amazon.com

Author inquiries and mail orders:
Finishing Line Press
P. O. Box 1626
Georgetown, Kentucky 40324
U. S. A.

Table of Contents

THIS IDYLLIC PHOTO GIVES NO CLUE   Photo/Karl Berger

I

Sitting on a grassy plateau
in the Austrian Alps
he in Tyrolean leather shorts
embroidered suspenders
she in a short sleeved middi blouse
and long skirt buttoned down the side

A cigarette dangles from Karl's hand
his left arm wraps around Lilli
a tinge of smile into the camera
softens angularity of jaw chin

Her head rests on his shoulder
arms extended she clasps her right knee
forearm against his thigh
willingly intimate yet
a distant gaze empties her smile

II

If a little boy dares look at her
he demands—what did she do

She says she won't see Karl again
he visits daily
She flees Vienna goes to Paris
His eyes cling closer than her shadow
His older brother wants to marry Lilli
Karl won't let him near
In calligraphy he woos her with his poetry

His forthright gaze vents
no heat from the fire within
Decades later she tells one daughter

continued

Their wedding night his harried taking
ensures she's never his waltz partner
merely his marionette
Outside the bedroom awed by her beauty
he'll do anything for her
she opts to be oxygen for his flame
it gives her light Stanza Break

III

Future photos scan
their arrival in the U.S. with year old Beth
two years later the unplanned
double burden

This idyllic photo emits no hint—
his flames lapping at the twin
resembling his wife
escalating rage at the three-year-old
for igniting him

Lilli's distant gaze
not caught again on film
is etched on her daughters' hearts—
lifting tea cup to lips
ethereal Mother's orbit is far

from his nightly sparks about the office
his fever if she serves a guest first
his two heart attacks while cancer eats his bowels
his death before sixty

Proudly she tells of his pursuit despite rebuffs
From this photo who would suspect
his grave is visited by no one

BEFORE THE BURNING OF FALL LEAVES

Two years after Father's release from Mauthausen
Anne and I are born in the USA,
the first and last of a generation.

Thirty minutes after Anne's debut
doctors drag me into the klieg lights.

Hearing of our double birth,
Father weeps. I am the second,
the extra he never forgives.

Swaddled in Mother's arms, Anne goes home,
I stay under incubator lights.

The one who swam with me
for three seasons
is held by our big sister.

Before pumpkins are carved,
Uncle Robert picks me up,

brings the stranger to that family of four.
Father, whose rage sputtered before he spent
three months next to crematorium chimneys,

does the goose-step into this little girl.
He does not brand me with numbers

but indelibly marks me *different.*
This fallen female weeps
from September to September

to September

PONDERING SHELLS AND COINS IN A DISH

I

One mollusk shell
plump as an African gourd,
a miniature conch,
one pierced shell waiting
to be strung into a necklace,
a white triangular chip
with amethyst stripes—

calcified sea-flowers,
fingerprints of the sea,
none duplicated,

and clusters of copper discs dull or glinting
their machined profiles in relief,
each identical.

II

A fraternal twin,
I have my own design,
wombed face to face, Anne and I
mirrored, bumped, squeezed,
thumb sucked, pulled and shoved
as one, as two.

She pushed out,
left so much room, I didn't
want to leave;
exhausted, I rested, but

forceps pinched, pulled;
Mother squeezed, pushed,
determined that I vacate home
eight months after I began
a struggle that echoes still.

continued

III

Twins, a double accident,
born in America,
foreigners
to their parents;

each without shadows,
neither followed the other,
wanted to be the other—

I envied some
of what she got:
cigar wrapper rings,
a Hop-along Cassidy outfit,
the nickname *Engie* Angel.

IV

I was the one
reshaped by Father's abrasions
incessant as ocean waves
yet my fingerprints remained
patterned as clam shells—

he could not erase them,
claim them as he had the rest
when he pinned me to the jetty,
lathered me with his foam.

Mother, clad as an angel fish,
unobservant as caviar,
scooted to the sea floor, refused
to let churning sand or water
ruffle her fins.

V
Plucked
from the sea,
parched by his heat;

stamped, riveted, flattened
into a profile-child
drilled, drilled, drilled—
a dull trinket dangling on his chain

THE GIRL I WAS

Four years old,
with his claw-arm he caught
my wrist, dragged me to the water,
my screams pealed as
my heels dug shallow ruts
in the sand.
He walked deeper
in. Ribs cinched against his torso, lids scrunched,
mucoused face pressed
against his chest, mouth pinched tight
to dam the flood, I hung
surfboard stiff.
Inhaling
thrashing waves, I hiccoughed,
coughed foam.
Flooding, flooding.
Then, as if he'd tamed a beast—
chin lifted, Father turned, slowly bobbed
to shore, dropped me
like a hefty suitcase.
Head drooped forward, wobbling,
I stepped around plaid
and striped blankets with bathers,
stared hard at grains of sand that shifted
between my toes,
scouring memory, I reached Mother talking
with my two sisters. My face
must have been illegible
as a shell, I sat, wheezed. Later,
in slow motion I ventured to the edge
of spent waves, filled my pink pail
with sand; its moist weight pulled
my right arm long. Softly I spoke
to my sisters about sand pies,
castles, and wheezed. How often
had I been caught? For each time
I was dropped, then forgot,

and was brave enough to play,
I'll pin gold stars to her hair,
      the girl I was.

FISH AND TACKLE

I am seven,
on the Greenwood Lake dock
and catch you,
my first/last fish.

My hook pulls you up by your lip.
Frantic flap, flap.
I can't stop
the swinging of my line,
can't touch, grab.
I yelp and freeze.

neighbor whose rod I use
removes the hook.
throws you back.
You swim free.

I retreat to three years old—
Father's long rod,
he reels me in.

I can't extract his hook.
I stop flapping,
am slack as a sleeping eel.
Father throws me back.

He casts more lines,
reels me in,
stunts my breath.

Ten, twelve, thirteen—
hooked, no struggle, no wriggle,
he throws me back.

Caught   caught
        caught

IN THE DIRNDL MOTHER SEWED

I start twirling
out on the front lawn,
nine-years-old, skinny and twirling,
my gathered skirt balloons into a pumpkin.
Quickly I twist left, right,
left, right, the hem lifting higher,
higher up my thighs.

My first open air dance,
my pre-teen exhibition of femaleness.
Exhilaration squelches shame.
I'm learning to be a peacock, happy that girls
have more glorious colors, fan their feathers wider,
strut more than boys.

What are my arms doing?
Oh yes, outstretched, my ballast,
my gyroscope, keeps me from tipping,
helps propel my twirls.

On this sparkling summer day
I feel ladyish in my flower-flecked,
ivory, scoop neck dirndl
with lilac piping. Barefoot
on the grass carpet, I spin
to oblivion.

GRANDMA DIDN'T TELL ME

Had she known English,
she still would not have told
me or anyone,
Grandpa, who died before I was born,
before Hitler marched through Vienna,
was strange,
a meager provider for their nine children;
dark bread with butter often their dinner.
He was too busy playing cards, telling jokes
at cafes. At home he must have been
mean. Mean to how many?
Uncle Hans and Father
hated him. Strange. He must have been strange.
Why else would Father be a pedophile;
Aunt Kate marry a pedophile; Uncle Hans never
have children though he loved them; their sister, Carol,
kill herself as her womb began to bloom; Aunt Grete
threaten suicide, remain shrunken by Aunt Kate's shadow?
Not one photo of him. No one ever said
his name. What did he die of? When?
At his graveside service did fictitious words
spin sugary masks as they did
at Father's, Mother's coffins?
The legacy of pedophilia—how many
generations back? Grandma didn't
tell me Grandpa's name.

FATHER SLAVERING

Rasp of his beard teeth on young vaginal flesh
he sounds like a pig at a trough
Tears surge but I hide them in my belly

Like snot dribbling from a snout
I cannot stem the flow
of moisture from below

Unspent tears swell my gut
as my seepage is tongued up
Voracious he eats quickly departs
to escape the sow he feels I've become

> I cannot marry
> a passionately sexual man
> I find the reverse of this werewolf—
> a gentle man whose passion
> begins outside the bedroom
> for music art
> for children and me

> His whistled tunes announce
> his arrival home from work
> Pushing me on a swing he sings
> *My Funny Valentine*

But those child-years of oinking—
sometimes I still hate
the swine in the mirror

That never-a-child girl
is still trapped inside

I've been gathering tools
to pick the lock
> When it's safe I'll let her out

JAGGED NIGHT

Inspired by painting #44
H Herschlag

A haloed moon outlines
jagged green mountains
against a royal blue sky,
and trees below as pointy
yet less menacing
than the neon-white teeth
of the huge mountain-dog
standing on moonlit boulders.
Her bulging yellow eyes two suns
in her squarish face
light the night sky
against predators.
Her arrow-like ears and tail
aimed at the moon,
her rectangular grinned mouth—
fanged warning,
protect the human fetus
inside her windowed womb.

Mother
where were you
at night?

SOME THINGS HE DID FELT FANTASTIC

His wet tongue
darting against my vulva
stroking my vulva
pushing my vulva forward back to the side
Oh my god
his lips surround-hugging   sucking

Willingly   I surrendered
pushed my torso
towards his mouth
tangoed with him
on taut violin strings

But without crescendo he left me
                      dangling
above

a bottomless want
for that delicate frenzied touch

The most despicable man in my world
Father the incest pusher
hooked me

On
Incest   Incest and more

Yet his lips on mine
his tongue in my mouth leaked arsenic
caused nausea to rise

Each muscle in his body my enemy
each hair and follicle another insult

Oh but his mouth on my vulva
his wet tongue careening carousing around my labia
pushing deep inside

Devil's Magic   Devil's Magic

NYMPHOMANIAC

My vagina shrieks
I hear my tunnel echo
feel the blisters pull
of yesterdays
from Father's gritty touch
Genitals
purposely roused and left remain
aroused
yawn for him
Those rare times when not
rasped by beard
or clasped in teeth
vagina wept
for tongue for him
and did not know why hunger
Leaping from his grave
he stampedes my sleep
My starving cry repeats
implies
there's something wrong with me
such sateless appetite

AN UNUSUAL APPETITE

Asked to climb inside the body
of a hunger-crazed lion to look out through his eyes,
I say No. Never. I don't want to see,
hear, feel his toying with his prey,
claws alternately retracted, extended,
swat, swat, swat; his tail flailing;
sandpaper-tongue lapping smooth
springbok underbelly, genitalia.

But then I shake my regal mane,
canines, incisors, gently, ungently, urgently
nip the fawn body stiffening to fear-rigid,
my shank hardens. A sudden shift,
her body pliant.
In a throbbing, frenzied rage
lion-me ejaculates.

Seconds later fawn flesh
and slimed vegetation cool my limbs,
I extract my claws
and pad across the den,
past the fawn feigning death,
enter my mate's lair, or
turn back, hunger renewed,
past the silent one, to the whimperer.

My tongue strokes her soft throat.
Her muscles, tendons tense, as though
the hardening shank of a rival.
Blood pumps into my groin, my paws graze
her sealed jaw, claws of my right paw
extend, snap the hasp of her jaw.

As I pump-pound the recesses of her mouth
her small teeth scrape me; each in, out,
like her too tight anus.
In a cascading gush I fill
the back of her throat then leave.

Sometimes,
the flash sight of this fear-frozen fawn
catching my scent
urges me on,
before her tawny body recedes into reeds.

In pre-pounce stance,
like a giant yawn, my legs unhinge
into a rapid stride.
Her fur in my teeth,
I shake my head left, right, left, right.

Then settle upon her—
frail bones splaying flat
as sapling branches of a banyan.
Her flapping heart,
birch leaves in a breeze,
flap, flap, her short breaths.

Then lift myself off.

OUR IMMUNE SYSTEM IS

Asthmatic bronchitis, infectious hepatitis,
ulcerative colitis, flu, typhoid fever,
costochondritis, kidney infections, flu,
osteomyelitis, peritonsillitis,
Sjogren syndrome, flu, hypoglycemia, rhinitus,
sinusitis, flu, thyroid cancer and diabetes—
the visible gifts from Father.

Protracted fear and rage,
the unseen killers inseminated into me—
their accrued psychic harm
is obvious to many.

Not so with brain damage—
prolonged stress induced
high glucocorticoid levels,
neuron loss in my hippocampus,
shrank the seat of memory.

Had I not buried fear and rage,
had I been brave enough to recall each rape,
had I murdered my psychic killer's power
by going public,
my immune system would not
have succumbed.

Letting buried memories
and feelings secrete hormones
to do their frantic work at night,
magnified, extended the rapist's
thrust long after his death.
Harm to mouth, vagina, anus,
was just the beginning.
Rapists invade each cell
and educate the body,
yield a doctorate in abuse.

Truces occur but scars remain
in the vestiges of our being.

Rape is a Grand Larceny
of the self
and the immune system,
but instinct for homeostasis
exists within us.
To retrain my nervous system
I do yoga, meditate, and
write, write, write.

IT'S TAKEN FIVE DECADES

Half a century
for her neck
to again become a neck

That soft flesh
denied kisses caresses
warmth of a turtleneck

No jewels
around her throat
it has had to be free

Of those two hands
that throttled her
three-year-old being

She still
sleeps on her side
arms crossed under her chin

But now in the cool
and warming feel of silk
she can parade chic

And her husband
dares kiss the curve
where neck and shoulder merge

Places his wide palm
below the back of her head
fingers curling forward

TEARLESS

Professor Marie I must ask
for the strangest favor
you know the origin of tears

Your heart was also bruised
adult weight on child
pressed into warp and weft

The other day I knocked
on your office door
pushed it open

Like a mother-bird
you flew up and wound
your wings around me
Falling into your smile I knew
if you taught me how to cry
I would not evanesce

In one try I learned to skate
to jump rope swing from a trapeze
I'm a serious student can you teach me

The first time is the hardest
they say   after that I think
I can do it on my own

For ten years I've practiced
at times a few drops
outside corners of my eyes

Terror
that hundred-mouthed giant
had sucked all the rain from the sky

Father's ban on tears
still parches that
dehydrated child inside

I must water her pinafore-years
poodle-appliqued-skirt-years
backwards-cardigan and slit-skirt-years

A flightless cassowary
dreaming of air currents
a desert cactus seeking floral status

Your arms your smile
might water my arid roots
make tears bloom as forget-me-nots

After receiving 3 awards as a
returning student as Hunter College

A BASKET OF CHOCOLATE TRUFFLES
as thanks Dear husband
professors, doctor and twin.

Herb, my man, you let me fling
tons of time and money at doctors,
on classes, on books, and patiently,
though you're sated on verse
you critique my work.
A homework-widower,
you cook, even clean a little,
and still think I'm beautiful.

Now Professors, I drop all
formality of title—
Dear friends, you have taught me
the subtlety of a curled leaf,
directness of a bearded iris,
the layering of rose petals.

Nondita, my mentor, you took me
under your wing, touched my hand,
said, *I know you can*, and promised
I'd add much to your class.

Bill, in body not always present,
afloat, enroute from Arizona to New York,
stuck in traffic, Laguardia to Manhattan,
or overwrought, and me, forgotten,
yet your spirit, selection of readings,
your pen, your voice long-distance
still strengthened my pulse.

continued

Marie, an adjunct, not paid to tutor,
you give me and give me gifts,
your thoughts, your heart;
my soul-sister,
you've taken me nearest my tears.

Richard, most recent member
in this adhoc quilting bee,
you tailored my corners with humor
and kindness, embolden my flame stitch
with golden yarn. You invited me
into your home at Hunter,
stitched epaulets to my muslin.
Together you all embroidered
awards around my scars.

I thank another, non-Hunter,
Ira, tenacious as a pit bull,
patient as Mother Teresa,
brave enough to venture
into the gnarled jungle of my mind.
You've combed smooth tangled roots,
plucked out toxic anger and pain,
clearing room for thought.

And thank you Anne, my twin,
paying for my first writing class
to baste my life with poetry,
kvelling when things go well for me,
for your joy in hearing my heart
relinquish its arrhythmic taunt.

Last but not least—Thank you
Hunter/English: Audre Lorde,
Blanche Colton Williams,
Sylvia Faulkner, for your work
and your accolades
that adorn my walls.

ANOTHER WRITERS' RETREAT

Again I'm the desert plant
in a lush temperate clime,
I'm a paper peony,
in a cluster of flowers
emitting perfume,
the blank page in a novel.

My hippocampus smaller
than an apple seed,
I remember less than
an Alzheimer victim.

I'm a woman without a tongue,
who cannot say if
I saw this film or read that book.
I could ask my husband
but he's not here,
so I sit and listen
to the absence in my mind.

I'm no longer a limping alien
like last time,
but I'm a member
without recall,
in a clutch of writers,
yet I find friends
who don't notice,
or accept me as I am,
a woman who writes from her heart,
not from her shrunken brain.

They say I am brave,
and like what I write.
I glide differently from them,
but I skim the water, then fly
in their V formation.

DEAR DR. OLIVER SACKS

You have studied the gray
that matters inside our heads.

Like an adopted child who needs
to learn who its real parents are,
I search for answers in my hunt
for most of my hippocampus—
when it shrank,
are neurons missing?
Can you help me on my quest?

In your circle of scientists
are any studying that small mass
that holds much of memory
and our GPS? Would they study mine?

I turn one corner then another
on a street, in a mall, a train station
and I'm more bewildered than
a three-year-old about
how to reach my destination.

I close a book that played
and fought with my heart,
and all but traces disappear
into the black hole
that sucks up each memory file.
After watching a movie with friends
I can discuss a few things,
but one day later it's as if
I had not seen the film.

As those orphans who seek the secret
of why their parents discarded them,
I yearn to know how it happened,
what acids or hormones gobbled up
my brain cells. Why do children

growing up in a war zone still have theirs?
Was mine decimated by the grenades
Father planted inside
my bedroom?

Most of all I want to know—
with stem cell research is there any chance
of re-growing my hippocampus?

SKELETONS DANGLING IN SLEEP

Terror propels me
out of bed
I check my neck in the mirror

Macrame flesh mud-brown center
taut dark strings radiating
to a wide-rimmed oval
is erased by daylight

I step cautiously
through each minute of the day
my body knotted sinew
my blood clotted jumping-beans

Last week I heard a poet—
tiny delicate braids
twined 'round her head

Angered by her cat
she grabbed its back legs
yanked them apart
pulled its tail straight out

About to shove
her lit cigarette
up its ass
suddenly she saw
her father's movements

Her sound-arrows
rattle skeletons
dangling
in sleep's closet

Each morning
their St. Vitus's dance shakes me
awake with bizarre thoughts
parching my mouth and eyes

I cannot stand
sounds that come from behind
my husband touching
the bottom of my spine

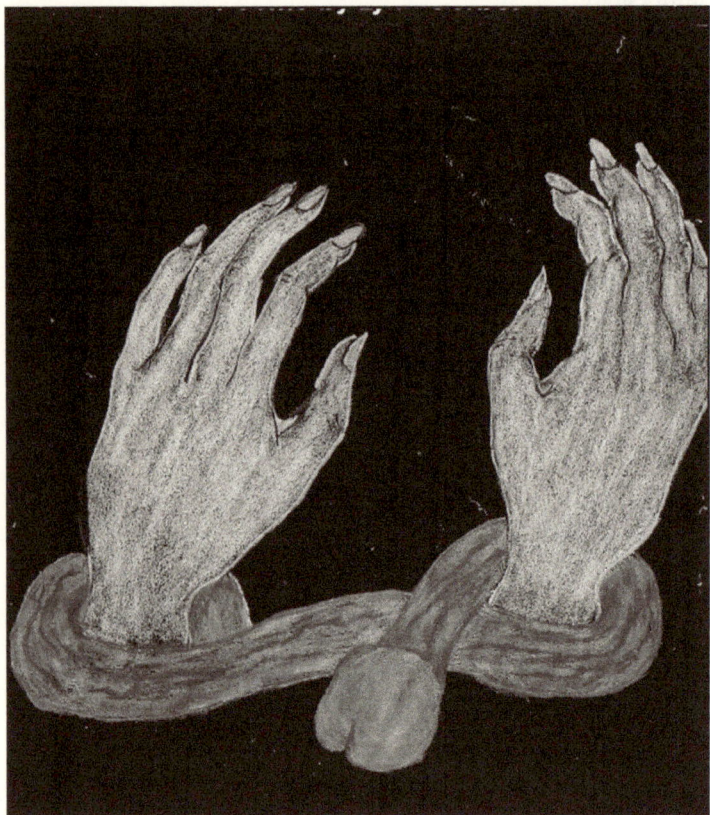

DAD'S PROPERTY

Me, his property
to do with as he wishes;
mind and body shackled
by his penis.

Feeling and thought stifled
by his wrath.
No space to hide,
no room for breath.

Death swiped him early,
providence seemed good.
Released from bondage,
by an open door I stood,

unaware his talons would grab
from six feet below.
Climbing toward health
I'm snared by Hell's claws.

While mirrors blazed fear
I hid from tyranny
then trampled through memory,
wearing a mask of normalcy.

Father still holds the deed
to much of me.

WHY DON'T DOCTORS KNOW?

Genie-Born 11/4/70

I

Genie, the wild child,
was found at thirteen, still in diapers
and tied to the potty in her bedroom,
no curtains, pictures, anything
for her eyes to eat.
My straps were internal,
around my mind and heart.
Skinny she was,
her feet could barely step,
legs bent so long on the potty.
Her arms worked, eyes sort of worked,
her voice was swallowed years ago.
Silent as me, I thought,
when Father did sex things.
Hers, no sex, just beatings. Mine did beatings
but I had the world outside my room, outside
my house. She had a potty. When they found
her, (miracle angel face, wide-eyed curious,
with caution-knit brow), she soon laughed,
her hungry hands touched, touched my pulse
as she, like a blind child, finger-surveyed
objects. Her eyes had never seen
anything but her body, four walls, a crib
she was often not allowed to sleep in, her
potty and bare floor. I think she too did
not know how, was forbidden to cry. Her ears,
never word-fed, could not teach her tongue *Ma Ma,
No.* All I want is to hold her, hug her,
rock her, as I wanted all
those years to be held. How naked
she must have felt, no humans except for
beatings. In my mother's womb my twin and I
shared fluid space, then shared a bedroom.
She was deaf and blind as the floral
wallpaper to Father's presence.

continued

When doctors took Genie in she filled a long shelf
with glasses of liquid, as do others like her.
Doctors don't know why. But it's their piggy bank
for future thirsts. Thirst hurts worse than hunger—
dry eyes hard to blink, no tears, mouth parched;
one's heart shrivels, its beat weakens. Doctors
are perplexed by her rabbit-walk. Let them sit
years on a potty, to learn, legs don't unfold
easily. Why don't experts hire an abuse survivor.
We know what they don't. NIMH funding gone,
institutionalized, stuffed back into a bottle,
            Genie how do you live?

                        II

Genie and I haven't met but we know wordless.
This is what she wanted to say—
Doctors are stupid. First they want me,
a newly discovered plant to study. They put me under
their microscope, dissect me; they get famous, tv,
radio, talk tours and government checks.
They talk gentle, give me clothes, food, toys.
Why no kids to play with, small ones so I feel big?
Every day they teach, teach words.
I only want my baby doll. Why don't they
teach me mommy things, hugging, rocking
my baby doll. They teach me how to dress,
tie my shoes. Now I teach my girl doll
all I know, even how to stamp her feet.
They give me tests they call games.
I don't care what shape fits into another.
I don't want electrodes on my brain.
I want a puppy who won't think I'm strange.
A puppy to wash my face. A puppy I can scold.
Why don't experts know? Why switch me from house to house?
I'm no postage stamp to be glued and sent anywhere.
They pretend they care, then send me to the woman

they call my mother. She never stopped the man.
Never untied me. Never took me out of that room.
Don't experts know, she's no mommy? That man
they call my father, he shot himself dead when
police found me. What does his wife know about hugs, songs?
Lullabies have words. They don't teach her mommy things,
just ship me back to her, then she too gets rid of me.
They test me for crazy. Adults are crazy or retarded. One says
I'm retarded, my brain waves show a sleep pattern. What
did he think he'd find in a starved brain? Where could it go,
trapped inside four walls with me? How long
can an empty brain stay awake? They say
a brain of a blind, deaf, mute child
well fed with touch, could stay awake.
Lock that expert in my room, no sound, no light, no touch.
Watch his fingertips grow bored. How long till his
well-schooled brain sleeps? These mind doctors,
when dollars stop they pack me off
to a foster home. I'm beaten for vomiting.
Doctors healed me then scissored me open.
Nothing will ever, ever again come out of my mouth.
Only my bottom. Why would I talk to retarded or crazy?
Maybe a puppy who doesn't make promises.
Experts are too dumb to know a puppy and I could talk
when no one is around to eavesdrop.

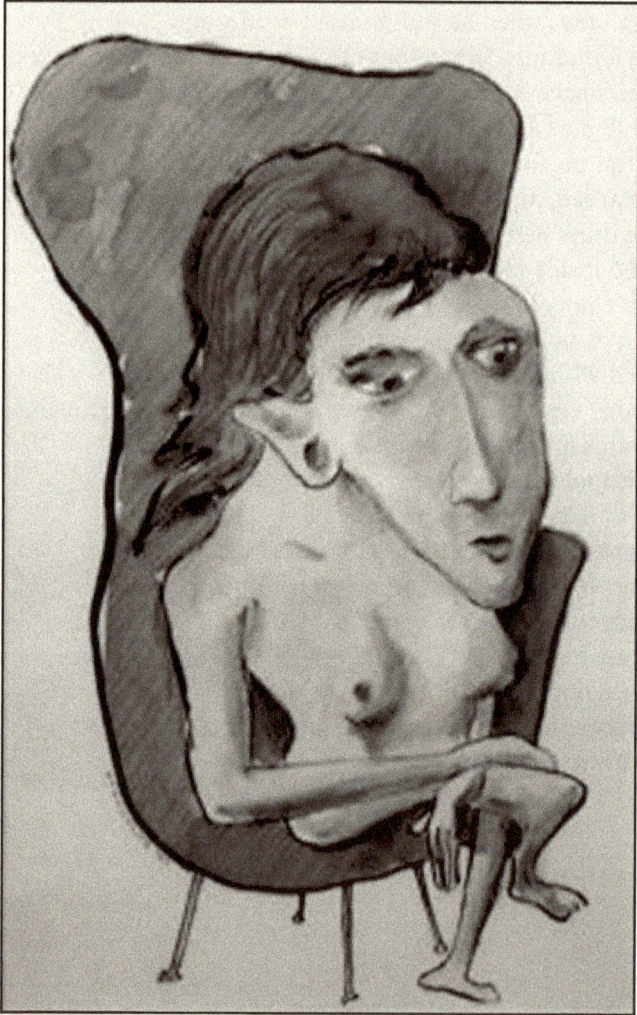

NUDE IN BLUE CHAIR

Inspired by painting #59
Distorted Female/H Herschlag

How did the painter know all this?
An accurate portrait
of my naked psyche as I sit in
the leather chair opposite my analyst—
my long dark hair offering
no cover
to my wounded-crimped brain,
my head ever-expanding
from memories exploding
into consciousness,
my jaw-line narrowed
as if by timidity and shame,
defenses stripped,
my thoughts and words stunted,
my hands' pretense at relaxation
exposed by my knees
locked in place,
my therapist's own
internal fires dwarfing my legs,
keeping me
stuck in a dichotomy
of liberation and diminution.

YOU DON'T UNDERSTAND
MY FEAR OF MURDER

Sometimes you ask *Why murder*
and seem to think
I'm distorting

Yes the spankings only stung my flesh
but were they preludes
to his raising the ante
After the choking I never knew
if Poker-Player-Father was bluffing
or was going to call in all the chips

If a gun is placed against your temple
once   that's enough
to always fear the next

Yet you ask
But he didn't kill you
why are you afraid of murder

I don't understand your question

YOU GOT IT

      Your Lord

And when you said *jump,*
I did,
when you said *No*
I cowered,
when you raised your arm,
I flinched.
Your Lord

Then I grew talons,
a beak and wings,
I tore at your flesh,
and stuck it in
to your eyes and ears.
      Your Lord

TO DEFEND I AVOID

Standing at the edge of tide-fringed waves
I can't shake my dislike for the sea

I avoid the stuttering gunfire of the world
I'm not informed don't read newspapers magazines
watch violent films

Childhood—one long loud lie of silence
Anything loud even Mozart rivets my spine

I hate the tuxedoed-lies of advertisers
their raised volume
I remote them mute or zap them off

Politicians spike truth
crooks klept businessmen abuse addicts act out
I fear the rejects' rage and the wrath of paranoids

But my *avoidance list* has shortened
a necklace or scarf can touch my throat—
I lie in bed belly up legs apart arms overhead
muscles relaxed

My mind can run amok on a page
my pen records from the gut
my paper-words scream hyena-loud

I may rent *Chinatown*—
before recall sucked my eyes dry
that film made me cry like a child
whose helium-balloon flew to the clouds

Perhaps I'll discard my pen name
admit who I am

WHAT GOOD IS A MIND WITHOUT A BODY
BLOSSOMS WITHOUT BRANCHES

I must gather my limbs
entwine them hold my mind
away from the reaper for a while

Plug wounds that ooze sap
post scarecrows to keep night's scavengers at bay
let dreams paint willow buds
forsythia unfurl sumac

I need the dark behind eyelids
a blanket of thoughtless snow
to silence childhood
feed me drop by melted drop
of nitrogen for renewal

Nine consecutive years of harvesting
row upon row of furrowed fear
thoughts elusive as wind-swept dust
and the shimmer of vermilion anger

Digging deep into my soil
depletes nutrients
my reserves are gone
it is fallow-time

WORDS

Mother's barely grazed my ears
Father's stung like wasps
parental words were never soft

Audible or written
they could puncture
the membrane confining recall

I crept into a cave of silence
muffled grown-up voices
songs music hid from books

Child-words were flannel
wound 'round me
layers between skin

and the chill of silence
till internal pressure hissed
childhood through my pen

and words formed flesh
for my adult frame
My eyes like two hungry mouths

sought poems of others
spun my notched words
into strands of tweed or silk

Now I wear audible taffeta phrases
plush velvet paragraphs
to color me outline my form

Substantiate my shadow

WRITE IN THE MIDDLE OF NOWHERE

My journal pen races across the paper, left to right, top to bottom. I free-write edge to edge. Margins are a waste of precious space. I need to use every inch or will run out of writing surfaces. So much jammed inside my head, waiting decades to pounce on the page, I can't squander even the top borders—sky for my writing. I need acres of white to fill with my atmosphere, topography, lightning rage, stalking monsters, yearnings for hammocked serenity. No room to record my hieroglyphs. I'd be caught inside my head, feelings swelling, festering, speechless again. I waste plenty but not paper. I recycle reams of it, all piled in the bin to be reused for shopping lists, note paper, wrapping paper, as raffia to stuff into cartons. Imagine a paper-less world—as if our tongues had been routed out. Our hidden selves would find no voice except on graffitied walls.

DEAR ANDREA

A victim of misdiagnosed post-partum psychosis

The moment I heard that you submerged
all five heads of your kids
in that porcelain womb
I wanted you DEAD.

Dead as I wanted my Octopus-Father.
Each summer he lashed his arms around me,
anchored me in the thrashing surf
of Jones Beach.

Then my heart heard yours
lost in the woods
torrid days, moonless nights,
crawling in brambled circles.

Your doctors held the compass
but like my mother, they pretended
you stood at the edge of the woods,
could walk the visible path
out.

Each refused to admit that a parent might,
but Father did,
you did.

A CURRENT OF HER OWN MAKING

She sought the familiar,
a man like her father,
stern and impulsive.

He raised her blood pressure,
her libido, brought her limbs to life,
and electrified her thoughts.

She assessed—some like sky diving
or spelunking. I'm a daredevil
with my partner.

She had not expected paranoia
to cross the surface of a pristine lake.
But he was sure she had given
her heart, at least in part,
to another.

Sudden as storm clouds over mountains,
his accusations drenched the still air,
his oar slapped the water
for emphasis, and to escalate
her fear as they drifted
on vast, isolated Lake Louise.
It snapped from his hand,
toward her.

Heart flapping, she grabbed the oar,
struck him once, twice, again. He fell
from the boat into the chilled fathoms.
As if on the ridge of Niagara
she frantically rowed away,
wondering where she could go
now that she had drowned
her life with rage.

SHE SAID, *YOU'LL RECOGNIZE ME; I'M VERY SHORT*

"So am I, five foot one and a half."
"That's a real height. I'm short."
"Well, I'll be wearing a black skirt
and yellow blouse, easy to spot. See you at noon."

On a Central Park bench an orthodox Jew wearing a schtetl,
and I who avoid religion, talk like sisters,
two crushed flowers that survived
numerous bulldozings of our terrain.

In a *New York Times* interview Bronia said,
". . . nothing induced me to cry. I want to
howl and howl, to infinity."
Hoping we could teach each other how to cry,
I sent my poems to her via the *Times*.
She loved them and is eager to learn.

Strolling to a cafe, towering over Bronia, I silently wonder,
did Auschwitz starvation determine her height,
a tiny 12-year-old cattle-carred into the camp?
She says, "My hunger began at 10. Looking a bit Aryan,
I became a smuggler, left the Jewish Quarter
to barter goods for my family's food. Then Auschwitz,
one slice of sawdust bread, one bowl of watery soup daily."

Steamy coffee mingles with July humidity. We hurriedly take
turns, disclose what cemented our tear ducts shut. I tell of
father's pseudo-drownings, the time he choked me. She says,
"At war's end, few children walked or were carried out of camps."
Numbers on Bronia's left arm are larger than any I've seen;
she's grown a lot since that branding. I'd have had my arm
untattooed, but incest survivor shame is imbedded below the skin.

Our exchanges, precise as radar, beam through the fog of tact.
"How do you know your sudden recall of child abuse is real?"
I answer, "My twin sister shared the room, she heard him in my bed."
Bronia says, "Your poems made me cry the second time I read them."
Her compassion moistens my eyes. I'm afraid to ask,
a few drops or real tears?

Hints of strain in Bronia's voice are smoothed by its lilt.
Her zest is contagious. She sounds like twenty, not seventy.
How did she keep her vocal chords clean
of the ashes she breathed?

She thinks being raped and beaten by a father from age three on
is worse than starving in filth and cold, facing likely death,
watching others be killed. I'm stunned, I'd thought

she might object to my connecting my horrors to hers.
Fear that my father might choke me again or drown me, she feels
built stronger dams against tears than what Nazis did to her.

Perhaps imagining the plight of others as worse
is a sliver of light in our boarded-up cell.

DOCTOR
WHEN YOU SPEAK

I sense your vibrations
know where you are

Always
in silence
Father entered
my bedroom
ten claws dragged me
across the bed

Always amid silence
his whisper-roars
punctured the air
with commands and threats

He ripped open my clenched arms and legs
did things and left

Doctor when you sit
shrouded in muteness
your paws pressed to your lips
I know soon I'll be chewed
and spat out

When you speak
the vibrations
are sunlight

Your hulking shadow
shrinks
reshapes
into a lamb

WHILE RECLINING
dentist's torso over mine
lip held/stretched
hands push press
deep in my mouth
ultrasonic drill
water's forceful spray

Oral surgery
brings IT back

Father forcing
thrusting
tearing mouth
flooding throat

I conjure up
therapist's sweet face
his sonorous voice

Pulse slows
dentist does
his dirty work

A HUMMINGBIRD

In silence
shy love-starved
craving a filial love
those first days
we nested for hours
on the tapestry
of my best friend's couch

Ever so slowly hunger
for contact sated
lips hands groins
reached for more

Sailor-boyfriend's kiss
upon my fourteen-year-old lips
traveled to my center

Purposeful as a hummingbird
Don ventured his wet tongue
into the bloom of my mouth

Gathering nectar
it flitted across my teeth
invited my tongue
to dance with his

My boy-man sealed his longing to mine
his arms the strongest of wings
tied us together

WIND AND SKY MY NEW SISTERS

I fly down the beginners' slope,
a hundred pound bird
with skis and two six foot poles.
Sun-warmed face caressed by wind,
eyes feasting on white
and shadowed snow—
a family outcast,
I race into Nature's arms.
Trees and sky my new family
healing as kisses
from my German shepherd
who whined and pawed Father,
pleading for him
to stop hitting me.
Nature, adds to my allies
her aerial bouquets
of sun-rimmed clouds,
her tree-studded land.
Speeding down,
down—gravity
fuels my power.
Entwined with the wind,
I traverse the hills,
intoxicated.
Skis lift me
from the corner
I crouched in at home.
The wind through bare trees,
and birds lure me
to sustained flight.
I am a new member
of a diverse
and large tribe,
always among family.

NO MATTER HOW MANY WARNINGS

She does not step gingerly
avoid deserted places
hold things up
to strong light

She is a dreamer of crinolines
ruffled curtains
moss between patio slates
bittersweet chocolate
on scalloped china

She won't lock doors
while the sun still shines
does not pull shades at night
She plans parties for moon-gazing

Semi-sheer curtains in an unlit room
armor enough for her
She seeks the permeability
of outside   inside

SILENCE FORGES MY TONGUE

Silence used to be
my whole bag of tricks.
Quieter than a sleeping marionette—
I couldn't say the wrong thing,
debate couldn't escalate.

Silence,
a fan that cooled my embers,
sent the mercury
of others soaring.

I couldn't fathom why,
but today fling silence at me
and I'll tongue-scorch you.

I won't be treated like
a falling leaf, a dust mite.
You'd better respond.

HOLDING MY BREATH

Lying across my queen-size bed
I inhale deeply, exhale slowly.
Tension from today's demands is bled.

Breath slowly sedates mind and body.
I focus on veins transporting blood
to arms, legs, digits, trunk, head.

Contemplating sunshine I inhale warmth,
and scan thoroughly as an MRI—
then out, out damn toxins, a raging wrath.

Purified by light sifting down from sky—
the monotony of counting 1 2,
while I exhale toxins, I wonder why,

3 4, 1 2 3 4, on silenced tongue—
feet, calves, knees, all sink in
to my mattress. 1 2 3 4 , muscles unwind,

a quiet peace flows through, I am calmed.
Then my audible vibrations of vuuuuuuuuuuuu
as I feel oxygen brighten blood in my veins.

In the hypnotic trance of less than 5,
pulse slows, I'm chilled but serene and alive.

EXTRAVAGANT AS TORTURE

Extravagant, like torture/S. Plath/Ariel

Extravagant as cancer,
as a musician on coke,
as a fanatic on religion—

Zealots can be truly imaginative,
their inventiveness for torture boundless.
What if they'd harness this brilliance,
to good effect?

Instead of flying jets into buildings,
they'd devise ways to provide food,
and create jobs for their people.

Both destroyers and builders—
Hitler, Osama, and Stalin
Einstein, Kepler, and Newton,
had extravagant minds.

Did you see fifteen-year-old,
Jack Andraka, when he won
the $75,000 Grand Prize
for his cheap, early-detection
pancreatic cancer test?

Jack's joy was ecstatic, exuberant—
his unconstrained mind
yields good for all humanity.

Regardless of geographical borders
Jack's work will diminish the extravagance
of illness.

MORE SENSITIVE THAN BRAILLE FINGERS

I teach
your
        silk-velvet-
cock
the contours of my face
        close my eyes
brush you
        with my lashes
Slide you
        against my cheek
around my lips   around
        lick the underside
up to tip
tongue-swirl gently
suck

Down my neck I guide you
        feed your cock
the map of my body
        draw a longitudinal-line
from my clavicle
south to navel
up east west
rub press
my nipples

As though connected
groin to mouth and sometimes limbs
nipples and clit bloom

Making sure your blind cock
memorizes
        I slide-press you
against my pubis clitoris

With my vagina's Ohs
       I scent you
tease you almost
         into around

I want to
       but can't wait
slide you
fit
A deep breath
motionless   silent
         before we shimmer

I HAVE A PASSION FOR PURPLE
and its paler cousins.
In my garden tiny flowers I named Lavender Lights.
Mid-November, amid dark ferny leaves
they spark the air like baby stars.
Purple, a seductive color,

a grown-up version of pink and powder blue.
Magenta, violet-powerful, urgent hues.
What's purple? Lilies, lilacs, orchids.
Ah, the color of sex.
When aroused, saturated with blood,
a purplish-red penis, vulva.

So we women paint our mouths in varied shades,
lift our erogenous zone from crotch to face.
Peacocks fanning our feathers,
we stretch color beyond lip edge
for that engorged look. Matte velvet,
shiny satin, wet and ready.

Life is sex. Food and sex. Delicious plums;
eggplant, earthy purple. Some tropical fish
and birds blaze purple, as do sunsets,
and broken hearts. Bruises, strident mauve
and rose, jaundice as they age and fade,
but re-emerge, like a shrub's second flowering,

when echoes fill the air. My doctor slips
into dead father's robe: Less than human—he says
of my meek retreats. Pointing his rage-purpled finger, he
says—*You wear layers of anger under ruffled blouses.*
Anger drives you into a mole hole, leaves me
on this prairie, hunting alone. Blame, ballooned

big as Father's rising hand when he hit, hit
hit. Then my doctor shorts me of time, so I slip
my purple-yellow self off the leather chair,
past his word-splattered walls.
Though I am a squashed plum,
outer skin ripped, inner flesh

flattened, oozing,
I am the yang of purple,
the underbelly of the rain cloud;
scars, like belts, hold in my pulp.
Early on I learned the trick of starfish,
will grow whole again.

THE HEAT OF ANALYSIS

I DOCTOR BOB

Poet, painter, parent-therapist with a third eye,
your Magritte-wit, flannel-gentleness win my worship.
I wear my shorter skirts, sandals, body hugging sweaters,
but you only give parental love. I'd never had any.
Not true. My husband is father/mother and mostly lover.
But from nightmares' knotted wool you skein my history.
Your only taboo after a year or two of unraveling my past,
you thwart more looking back, and point me forward, only forward.

Such throbbing in my beaten body.
Too many wounds reinfected by momentary glances.
They need lancing but you refuse. More white cells brew.
Death's vice cinches my lungs, as when Father's weight
pressed me into my mattress. Now I'm months housebound
by Suppression sucking out my air. No, your love is not enough.
After childhood, Truth is the only antibiotic.

II DOCTOR IRA

In your office, like dust my voice falls into corners.
Sometimes your velvet questions soften my scabs,
my blood sheds white cells. Other times your ears are perked
towards me, your teeth snip your nails, your eyes glaze,
or you spit quills at me. I say, Your loss of control,
like my father's, dangles, a dagger hidden in a chandelier.
I cajole myself, I'm not here for approval. It's facts I want.
But without your arms, more motherless, it's still too dangerous to cry;
new scabs mound my wounds. I retreat further into
the leather chair, numb to the barbs you flick into my
parent-bereft rage. You prick my orphanhood
yet scowl like a disobeyed parent.

continued

I don't trust the minute hand of my watch
but my car radio repeatedly confirms, you start 3 minutes late
yet give the full 45. Then you start late but end on the hour.
I admit I can't, but my twin tells her doctor sexual details,
past, present, and fantasies. You again say,
She didn't have sex with her father.
Not—Her father didn't have sex with her.

You swat with claw-words, then retract them:
You retreat so that I will, to avoid dealing with things.
Of course I don't have to retreat, that's my responsibility.
I cajole myself, I'm not here for approval, but red welts linger.

Last week your silken words sooth me,
You've changed, are more centered, less guarded,
speak louder. A moment later your lids droop.
Am I putting you to sleep?
Yes. What happened? As soon as I said you're more vibrant,
you put me to sleep. What's going on?

And on rare days, stars or tides induced, I feel all woman,
then you hide behind the curtains of your eyes.
Yesterday, *Were you a virgin when you married?*
My jaw drops. Knotted words tie my tongue to my teeth.
Oh, for a moment I forgot, as though you were normal.

Last month, *I've been thinking, your withdrawals make you meek,*
less whole, less than human. This makes me abuse you.
Makes is the wrong word. I'm in control of my behavior.
But I wouldn't attack a vital person.
Is that what made you more of a target for your father?"

III SELF-DEFENSE

I should shout—Father's choking me when I was three strangled my spunk.
I'm cardboard-flat only in your office. Vitality is magnetic.
I must prevent attraction. Besides, buoyant, I'll forget
to keep my fists raised.

Unlike Father, Ira wants open combat. At last I assert:
You plug my tear ducts. I can't surrender to a non-ally.
You don't know how, are unwilling to parent me. Your quills hoarse my voice.
Your demands of surrender yeast intestinal pain and yank out my hair.

Rather than admit mother's hands, eyes, voice never caressed me,
I surmised I didn't know how to feel her touch. Decades later
I deny your antiseptic heart till I read a sexual abuse expert. Frawley
blows your menthol against my eyeballs. I console myself, I've learned facts.
But my chocolate-hunger grows with each session.
For months I complain but you don't see your cold reflection in my eyes.

Deprivation, accusation, mirrors of childhood sometimes light the fuse
that set off the erotic bomb, a craving for cruel and sensuous touch, but
the more your quills puncture like Father's, the more I need to escape.
Before I'm bald and my intestines explode I must leave. At 12,
I was chained to home, but your tether can't hold me.

And now a wolf springs at my throat, thyroid cancer,
amid my wrenching last week's sessions. The pre, and I'm sure
post op nightmares, going it alone because you shoved me out the door
while conning yourself that I'm a quitter.

You were the first and only one undaunted by Father's sadism,
a detective with woodpecker determination and heron patience
plucking out information. For that I owe you. But for 5 1/2 years
of my biweekly, then triweekly sessions, from your errors, like a mole
you hurriedly burrow away and stay in your tunnel.

Perhaps you see me as, fear me as, the siren in a red dress.
To combat my misconstrued retreats you skunk the air with rejection,
while I think myself strange, never learning to cry.

Moments when your x-ray vision decodes me, my heart and groin yearn
to reach across the room. But mostly you wear goggles as you spin
this temptress into rags of reticence. How can I say—You thwart

continued

my outstretched arms, my childish clinging? How can I surrender
to you as a ballerina, trust you'll catch me if I cry?
You deem this resistance, an insurrection to your delving,
my desire to demean your erection.

But you make yourself impotent,
not examining your shrinking my vocal chords, blocking my tear ducts.
Doctor, why no comfort-words to unclog my river of thoughts and tears?
You choose bat-blindness, refuse to use your sonar to sense your
closeness to father: abuser, blamer, feeling innocent.

Yes, you finally succeed tapping into the aorta of my anger.
Ceiling-high, I heap your unlove on top of Mother's and Father's.
My anger yeasted by hurt and want brews hotter than sex,
has the power of bonsai roots fighting against constraints.
So I slam therapy's door, hammer it shut with penny nails
and a dead-bolt lock. I won't ever offer myself up
for more rejection, for my doctor to say
about my coaxed reticence, less than human.

IV ON THE OTHER SIDE OF YOUR DOOR

In my absence we both grow more real. I gain moxie. No longer fearing
you'll ransack me for my anger-words, I send this crow-voice poem
and attached note: Fear-tied, my tongue never lacerated Father,
but today, through the teeth of my pen I hiss
and spit my acid at you. I stamp this poem and post it,
hoping it eats holes in your goggles,
erodes your denials, and gouges pitted scars
in your ego's complexion.

Regretting the way our mutual efforts end, you read my stridency,
offer one, then a couple more non-fee meetings
to iron some of our creases.

My voice floats up from the corners—Your lack of connection
inflates your perception of my writing skills—compensation
for making me cower instead of expanding my vocal repertoire.
In response to my unreturned fondness for you, you say, *That was
an unfortunate lack of mirroring.* ...... *You deserve the best.*

No longer your patient, you toss embracing words at me
as you close your door. But my words blaze red.

THE JOURNEY

Inspired by a painting
by H. Herschlag

Cliff shadow and my shadow
in this monochromatic world,
my only companions;
not even a tree or dog,
just barrenness,
insurmountable black hill
jutting up from
an expanse of blinding white
wilderness,
desert of singularity,
changeless,
except for the growth
and contraction
of our shadows,
yet I walk forward,
perhaps to meet something
at the horizon.

THE SPIRAL SUN—

Inspired by
painting #45
Spiral Sun/H Herschlag

Speckled as a grapefruit
on the rippled lake-mirror
inhabited by croaking frogs

My thoughts flap—
a sail in a halting breeze
waiting for a steady wind
to inform my eyes

Potent as a magnet
the steel-gray water
pulls my eyes to a dream image
shimmering on its surface

Blonde hair auburn-veined
piled high as an erect phallus
on Mother's head

Sunlit it smolders a warning
more menacing than
her hooded eyes
bared teeth

The heat in her—
the rage at the daughter
she does not want

EXCLUDED

Grainstacks in Bright Sunlight/Monet

A falling rainbow stretches itself
across the horizon,
blending into dawn's dense fog,
painting grain-stacks and meadow—

This softly colored world invites me
to lie against a purply-brown
almost-tent of grain,
but the cool morning dew repels me.

The newly risen sun's halo
on trees and stacks promises warmth,
but an unwelcome chill
clings to the fog.

Implying a lapse of time—
Monet's shadows are cast in two directions,
but the air remains damp,

continued

leaving me a bystander,
a mere observer
of this dream-like beauty.

EGRET SAYS—
DON'T BE DECEIVED

Photo/J Hershlag

Twinned by the marsh,
we make a great
spectacle.
Neck stretched,
I peer through mottled water
in search of fish.
I look innocent
as a sleeping child,
still as a rock,
then swift as an arrow
I grab my catch.

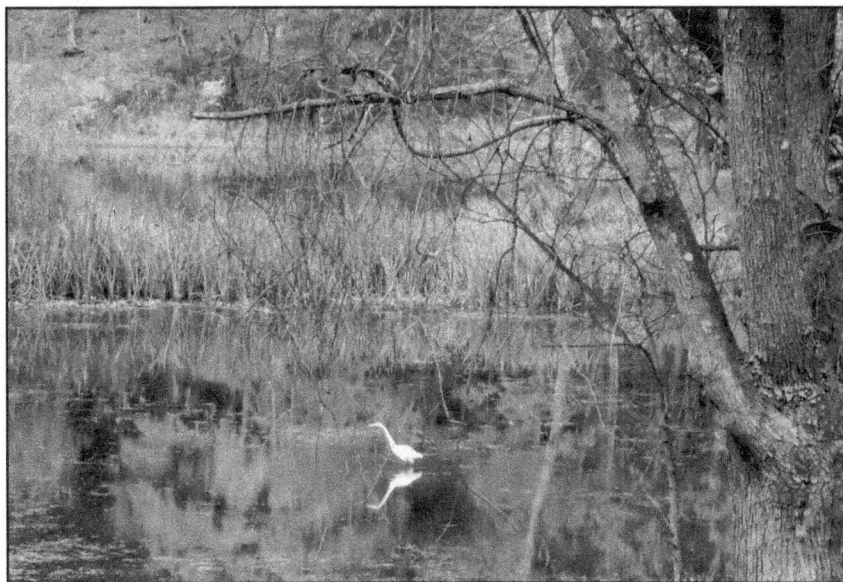

MOTHER NATURE SAID—

Photo/J Herschlag

You, graceful and stunning blue heron,
with wings wide enough
to float you on air,
and a giraffe-long neck,
you cannot have all the assets—
so she taxed your voice,
a hoarse croak
that startles onlookers.

THE MOST IMPORTANT SEX ORGAN
IS THE BRAIN

Dr. Reiner

Mind over matter?
I can't walk on coals,
but can meditate away much pain.

And I agree with Dr. Reiner,
our brain can enhance
or deny body sensation.

Eyes open to minutia—
beauty abounds in the smallest surprises,
leaf-shadows on a stucco wall.

Especially on days of sadness,
watching a bee explore a flower
uplifts me like Mozart.

Walking in his garden, Pablo Casals said,
The beauty of a rose can make me cry.
Such concentrated focus is there for our taking.

Do your own tally, most calculations
come out on the plus side if one has
shelter, food, and lives in a non-war-zone.

I try, when my husband makes a crumbly mess,
to think of the X-rated grilled cheese sandwiches
he creates for me, better than the best panini.

It's almost our 50th—the thought of a solitary life
for either can cause gut panic, but family and
friends also pollinate our hopes and dreams.

When body chemistry subverts my health,
I bribe my brain—there's an RX
to counterbalance much suffering.

continued

Some say *Mellow out before sleep,*
but our multi-talented brains sleuth through
dream-fog to problem solve, intuit, and invent.

I hope to keep my mind dementia-free,
pleasured by trees, birds, dried blossoms,
clouds, people, and the morphing moon.

A SABRA AND AN ACACIA

Inspired by painting
Rabbi Y. Herschlag

We look as different as a cat and dog.
Both of us are spiny and like
the same arid soil and desert clime.

I drop my leaves in winter's cold
while the sabra keeps its succulent pads.

Different as we are—
unlike warring tribes,
we grow side by side
sharing the Judean Hills.

CONCORDANCE

Oedipus and the Sphinx
Gustave Moreau's painting

Unafraid of the directness
of her firm pointed breasts,
her penetrating gaze,
he searches deep into her eyes,
swims in the safety of their openness.

Her nipples aimed toward his lips,
gently her eyes rock
the fever in his heart.
Lullabies plait her hair,
geometry sculpts
the swirl of feathers and tiara.

His muscular nakedness
smelling her power, undaunted,
he stands at ease.

His left leg, slightly bent,
lowers his hip in silent answer
to the weight of all four claw-retracted
lion feet, their fleshy pads resting
on his thighs and ribs.

A pair of eagle-wings
sprout from her shoulders,
extend skyward, form a pillow
for her arched head.

His deep-set eyes lap up the shimmer
on her glazed skin rouged by yesterdays' setting suns,
shyly he lets his eyes speak into hers;
her breasts echo his yearning.

Unafraid of the animal within
her, him, Oedipus tilts his head toward the crowned sphinx,
her heart floats into his, his into hers.
They remain a few inches apart,
air between them scented lilac.

WITHOUT MY TWIN WHO WOULD I BE?

Now I wonder, the miracle of survival,
like my friend hiding in a haystack
as a Nazi searched with a pitchfork.

Without Anne I'd be a spinster
or in an institution.
We shared a womb, a crib, stroller and playpen.
We had tugs of war, hair pulling, but mostly
we gibberished, and intertwined limbs.
I was the runt, Anne, my protector.

Candies didn't exist in our house
but mounded dishes at our Aunts'.
Shy, arms pressed tight to my sides,
I couldn't stretch to reach the crystal bowls.
Anne took enough for both.

When Father grew meaner,
my behind too sore to sit on,
Anne shut out sound so hard,
her ears oozed pain and pus.
I drenched my pillow with whispered sobs.

We retreated. She into blindness, deafness,
I into numbness, or vanished
till he left our room,
and breath re-inflated me.
My mind forgot,
my body did not.

Then teenaged boys, hugs and kisses—
I held cupid's arrow, had wooing power;
weapons of love strengthened me.

continued

Incested girls often trade in their minds
to keep their bodies; we can't keep both.
I kept my mind;
my body went miles away.

Sixteen years under Father's rule,
then merciful death interred him.
Infections fierce as Father,
sentenced me to hospital stays
till I listened, penned and spoke.

It took decades to turn
fluorescent lights on home,
and remind myself—
Anne and I taught each other
the touch of feathers, of sunlight.

MY WRITING GROWS WILD AS A VINE

Speedy and tenacious as bittersweet,
it strangles blossoms of polite charm that concealed
toxic flora in our *Home Sweet Home,* thriving beneath
lovely lace doilies, Austrian crystal and Rosenthal China.

Last week my older sister cut
a fable out of invisible cloth:
Mother daily hung all our bed linens out to air.
I was embarrassed; our neighbors never did that.

My twin and I know
only when washed
did the linens hang from a clothesline
in the garden to be bleached by the sun.

Did big sister spin this yarn
on the wheel of her mind to cleanse
the stains she and Mother refused to see
that Father and brother-in-law spilled

on a daughter's sheets.

THE METAPHOR OF ILLNESS

Submission beaten into my young body,
self-defense ringed out of my neck,
by age three I lost all tools to oppose.

      * * *

Mt. Sinai's Chief Dental Surgeon
supervises, as his student hacks
at my impacted wisdom tooth.
Dr. Cranin returns to see the progress—removes
the wrongly inserted intravenous and corrects it.
Occasionally he checks back in;
ninety minutes later he completes two extractions.

A month of days crawls by,
my mouth still opens less than an inch,
Dr. Cranin says, *It's just psychic. Chew bubble gum.*
Two more months, two more dentists, a jaw specialist,
no healing or diagnosis.

I sink deeper into pain and my tear-soaked pillow,
assessing myself mentally ill.
Zombie-like I cook and care for two preschoolers.
As fall tinges summer, throat pain rivals jaw pain,
my voice peeps like a chick's. I drag one heavy
leg in front of the other, to my internist.
A blood test—instant hospital admission.

An x-ray technician pries my swollen jaw apart,
places film on the wound. The head and neck surgeon says,
You have a fifty percent chance of surviving
this jaw bone infection that has spread.
If you make it through the next twenty-four hours
you'll soon walk out from here. I won't get involved,
but you should sue the dental surgeon.
Don't ask me to testify. I become incoherent for two days,
than rally toward health.

* * *

Two decades later I discover,
my body knew what my mind buried—
that student's assault echoed Father's oral rapes
when Dr. Cranin, like Mother, absented himself.
More than tears, that surgeon incited a flood
of white blood cells that nested in my jaw.

WINTER LURES ME

Clouds, static as chess pieces,
pretend to be mountains above
the rolling hills; snow-topped rocks
in the glistening black brook
look like amorphic marshmallows;
sun glistens electric wires
into strands of 24 carat gold.
Too lazy to trudge through deep snow,
we go for a photo search in the car.
Brown lamas now are more vivid
in the albino landscape than the white lamas
on the green lawn always demanding notice.
The folk-art rooster next to the red shed,
seen against the white canvas,
pops out more than when
surrounded by green, or ambering grass.
These miracles make me forget I am shivering,
standing knee-deep in snow
that seeps into my sneakers
as winter lures me in.

ANALYST

Ink Drawing/H. Herschlag

Your outlined face,
blank as an empty page
that I'm supposed to write
my free-associations on.
I dare to attach meaning
to your eyes, your questions,
and wonder—
do I paint a face
onto you or
does your face
impose itself onto me?

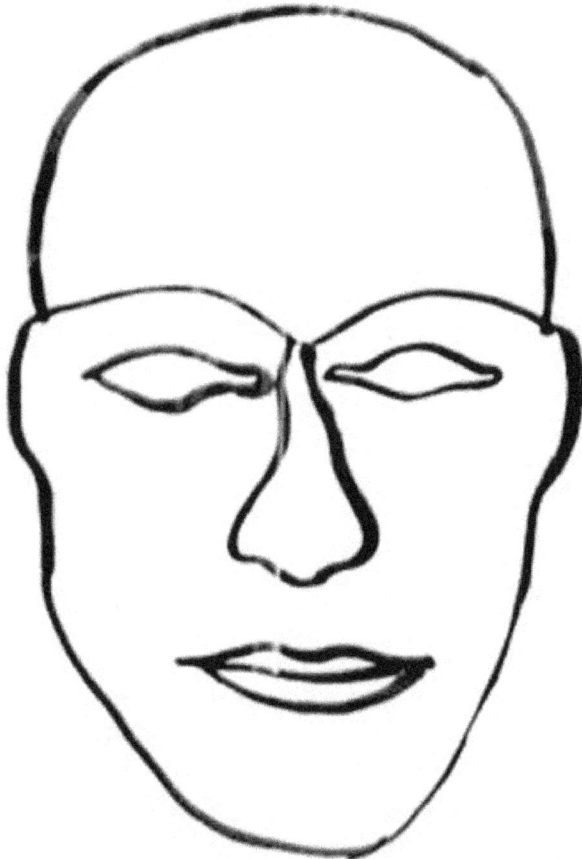

BEAUTY IS IN THE WARPED LENS
OF THE BEHOLDER

Novakchott, Mauritania—Islamic women
of northwest Africa, the fatter the better.
A new campaign hopes to stop
the force feeding of young girls,
whose beauty, like diamonds,
is determined by size—the fat
hanging from their arms.
Starting at age 4, 14 gallons of camel milk
are forced down Mey's gullet daily.
Vomit, she's beaten;
refuse, her fingers are bent back.
By 10 she can't run; her mobility
decreases yearly, like Chinese girls
with bound feet, like bone-corseted
European women wanting the admired
13 inch waistline, fainting from lack of air,
like Taliban females in Afghanistan,
mobility denied by decree
and their mandatory burkas,
only their eyes naked, but thickly, darkly outlined,
while their husbands dream of heaven with 72 virgins,
like Ubangis, both sexes with pierced lips
stretched around flat wooden disks.
Congolese men seek scarification
to make skin look embroidered,
western men use anabolic steroids to increase muscle mass,
4-year-old girls already want a Barbie Doll figure,
their mothers risk cancer with silicone breast implants,
remove ribs for the hourglass figure,
bulimics crave food then vomit to be thin,
anorectics starve themselves while feeling fat,
and hair, dye it, perm it, straighten it, bleach it, or,
shave it as Hassidic women do to avoid tempting other men,
while some of their husbands frequent whore houses.
Even the Tammy Bakers (bouffant hair, makeup-cartooned face, and
lashes bunched by mascara) are dissatisfied with what has been given them.

Why do men feel impotent, women feel undesirable?
Oh to be a male bird boasting colorful feathers,
strutting, dancing and singing to seduce the girls;
oh to be a female bird,
desirable just as they are.

INTRANSIGENT WOUNDS

At home the child was unnoticed
as a dust mite
except when sought
for the punishment of her flesh.

Then came her lover-husband's
amazing gaze at her,
so why does she stay so hungry
that even vats of chocolate
don't sate her?

A teacher once said—
After a parched childhood,
learning to absorb hugs
remains elusive as a candied apple
dangling on a string.

Early love-hunger
persistent as dandelions,
remains un-fillable.

Decades have passed
yet she feels truncated—
partial amputation of her psyche
echoes with phantom pain.

TRAPPED

My ten day silent meditation retreat—
remnants of old wounds shout
through shafts of body and mind

A groin pull for three days thwarts sleep
        too much lotus sitting?
Next salivary gland pain
        another stone?
Next simultaneous knife pains
vagina rectum
        hemorrhoids?

Next a glass bomb explodes
in my vagina Two words fly
into my brain Japanese beetles

      *****

The summer my big sister got polio
paralyzed trapped in an iron lung
I was seven and trapped
and murdered hundreds of beetles

My sister's polio transformed Mother
to a statue staring into empty space
celibate I'm sure she thought sex ugly

Beetles ravaged roses in our garden
ate holes in their velvety flesh
I hammered nail-holes in metal lids
and trapped them in jelly jars
mayonnaise jars

They smothered slowly
in their hard dark shells
in a crowded glass coffin

Each beetle was Father
For what felt like glass shards
rammed in my vagina
I smothered him hundreds of times
in jelly and mayonnaise jars

A FEW WORDS AND BITS OF DESSERT

Because you listen with more accuracy
than tape recorders without nuance
and you often join puzzle pieces
before I recognize their implied shape
because my ghosts of rage and terror don't
shut your eyes or ears to my unchildhood—

with you as witness I grow brave enough
to enter an unknown land of silence
A ten day meditation retreat—No
talking reading writing radio no
eye contact Obedience strict attention
to my leader twelve hours a day

After six days of déja vu submission
surrender installs a larynx in my flesh
Groin shrieks (from sitting lotus?) soon
an explosion of glass splinters in my
vagina It roars louder than ten lions
On the eighth day of silence I listen

to the child screaming and pushing inside
the twenty-seven foot tunnel of my guts—
silent admission anesthetizes pain
Did admission and I expel Father
But a month later I tell you I again need the speed
of a cheetah to out-run Father Pain comes
and goes a common-law-partner quieter

Daffodils now yellow the ground I claim—
three months ago expelled into the open air
and we have transformed Monster into
a dead man disenfranchised as vapor
Because you are so good at shaping smoke

into mirrors I now see more clearly
but still need time to break the night-habit
yet expect my pit bull jaws to unclench
And since I'm a good dessert maker here for you
chocolate-dipped apricots and halvah

A PACT FOR LIFE

In a decades-long stretch across the soil
an elm reached its trunk
to another, then gently wound
itself around her.

Making sure not to deprive her
of sunlight, he bent west,
almost perpendicular
to their coiled selves,
leaving ample space for each
crown to reach its potential.

Herb lifted me from the dank shade;
in our long-term embrace
we widened each other's vistas.

His melodies coaxed me
to reach skyward, and laugh
with the sun dappling me.

In the fertile soil of companionship,
with plenty of space to be wreathed by light
still modestly crimped by bad weather,
some of our buds reach their potential.

I DREAM OF IRISES

purple as amethysts,
crowning long thin stems,
rimming a pond soaked jade green
by reflected plants and trees.
Patches of sky-blue also shimmer
the wet jeweled surface.
Spring invites
my camera and me
to scan wood and hill
for more beauties
to adorn my sleep.

A LULLABY AFTER CRIMSON FALL

Ambered grasses sprout tall
beside the mown green lawn—
a buffer between flatness,
jutting pine,
gold and orange maple,
and leafless trees
against a colorless sky.
Wide swaths of muted shades—
an interlude
before winter's sleep.

REBEL

She leaps out
from the austere cubicles of home
overflowing with dry ice
and finds a mate unwilling
to let go of childlike play.
His daring to venture into silly
leads them to frolic in clover.
She pinches sage between her fingers
to sate her awakened sense of smell,
and puts gold starflowers
behind her ears, in her pockets.
They holds hands, leans torsos apart,
and spin, falling to the grass
like three-year-olds.

I AM ONE PROUD LAMA

Just look at me
recently shorn,
white as a daisy.
Haloed by sunlight,
I offer my profile
to be captured
by your gaze.

Yes Lama,
my guilt recently shorn,
I moved from shadow
to sunlight,
from hiding in a cave
to a solo aria
on a white paper stage
to also be warmed
by the gaze of others.

SUMMER AND WINTER IT'S MY STAYCATION

Staycation—coined in response to gas prices
making travel prohibitive

My magical home
beside a small lake,
wooded on two sides—
each dusk bats feast
on mosquitoes,
leaving me bite-free.

On my back deck,
I'm serenaded by brook
splashing over rocks,
especially as clouds open their fists;
after, the happy hunt for worms
and the air is punctuated by birdsong.

Clear blue above,
hundred-year-old maple and oak shade me
early morning and late afternoon.

I've painted my garden
with high-climbing clematis,
crimson and violet salvia,
blush of peony and mime-white Shastas.

Primroses, the finest of weeds,
not pesky like dandelion—
light up my flowerbeds.

When trees undress for winter
and blossoms are a dream long gone,
sculpted forms of willow
and jagged armature of sycamore
play against the sky.

continued

Some days, the neighborhood draped
in bridal snow, I'm forced to wear boots
to inspect the myriad designs:
bouffant bushes, a hillock re-frozen
satin-sleek, with a wind-moiréd bridal train.

Except for minor infringements—
ant infestation at doorways,
mice infiltrating my garage,
squirrel migration into attic,
this is an ideal bed and breakfast,
lunch and dinner.

In tandem to psychotherapy, in her mid-forties, **Ms. Herschlag** finally put pen to paper to release the demons within, and shortly thereafter she used a camera for the first time, as solace, capturing the beauty of nature. Now an award-winning photographer of iconic New England scenes, some photos are included here with her poems, as are ekphrastic poems inspired by her husband, Herbert Herschlag's paintings, or museum paintings..

As Jane says, *Witnessing ones history through analysis and journaling heals, and going public at readings enhances recovery. I became addicted to writing poetry. When still afraid to voice memories offeelings, the secrecy of pen to paper encouraged me to let it all out.*

Curiosity awakened, and having a sudden yearning for more education beyond her AAS degree from the Fashion Institute of Technology in NYC, Jane went to Hunter College. As a top student with a double major of English Literature, and Women's Studies, and as a graduate student in the M.A. program at City College in New York she won many awards. Jane won the Sylvia Faulkner Award; Honorable Mention/Poet in New York Prize; Hunter College Dept. of English/ Blanche Colton Williams Fellowship, and 2nd Place/Audre Lorde Award; she was a semi-finalist in Radcliffe's 2000 Bunting Fellowship, and a semi-finalist in Elixir's 2006 poetry contest.

Jane's poems are published in five anthologies: *Changing Harm to Harmony; Queen of Swords; Rising to the Dawn; The People's Press;* and, *Writing Our Way Out of the Dark.* Her poems appear in many university presses such as: *Manana; Negative Capability; Onion River Review; Graffiti Rag; Mediphors; Psychopoetica; Salonika;* and, *The Returning Woman.* Her docu-poetry collection, *Bully In The Spotlight,* was published in 2007 by Pudding House Publications.

Ms. Herschlag taught creative writing at P.S. 22 in Queens, NY. At Escape to the Arts—the Writer's Voice at the Regional YMCA of Western CT she taught creative writing to children and adults. She curated the Open Mic reading series for the Writer's Voice at ESCAPE, and for seven years, at the West Side YMCA in NYC. She has been a featured reader at cafes and libraries throughout NYC, as well as on the radio and Manhattan Cable TV. She moved from Queens to Connecticut in 2003.

Jane also participated in numerous writing retreats, and won scholarships to Skidmore College; Wesleyan University; Juniper Summer Writing Institute; and, Fine Arts Writing Center. A book promo for her yet to be published memoir *Tearing Off The Covers* can be viewed on YouTube; after the title in quotes, add Jane Berger Herschlag, then click on the black & white photo of 3-year-old twins.